The Very Best Christmas Ever!

Emilie Barnes

WITH ANNE AND ELIZABETH BUCHANAN

Illustrations by Michal Sparks

HARVEST HOUSE PUBLISHERS
Eugene, Oregon 97402

The Very Best Christmas Ever!

Copyright © 1998 Emilie Barnes and Anne Christian Buchanan
Published by Harvest House Publishers
Eugene, Oregon 97402

Design and Production: Garborg Design Works, Minneapolis, Minnesota

Library of Congress Cataloging-in-Publication Data
Barnes, Emilie.
    The very best Christmas ever! / Emilie Barnes; with Anne and
Elizabeth Buchanan; illustrations by Michal Sparks.
           p.   cm.
    Summary: Directions for making various Christmas decorations,
gifts, and foods accompany the chapters of a story about a group of
friends preparing to celebrate Christmas.
   ISBN 1-56507-905-1
    1. Christmas decorations—Juvenile literature. 2. Christmas
cookery—Juvenile literature. 3. Christmas—Juvenile literature.
[1. Christmas decorations. 2. Christmas cookery. 3. Christmas.]
I. Buchanan, Anne. II. Buchanan, Elizabeth. III. Sparks, Michal,
ill. IV. Title.
TT900.C4B37   1998
394.2663—dc 21

                                      98-3111
                                      CIP
                                      AC

Special thanks to Pam Farrel for allowing us to use her wonderful "You're an Angel" ornament idea.

Printed in Hong Kong

98 99 00 01 02 03 04 05 06 07 / IM / 10 9 8 7 6 5 4 3 2 1

14.99

CONTENTS

How the Christmas Club Got Started

Hi, I'm Emilie Marie, and I want to tell you about a great idea my friends and I just came up with.

We're going to have a Christmas Club!

It started when my best friend Christine and I were talking about all the things we want to do. Christine wants to decorate her room for Christmas. I want to make my own gifts and cards and go caroling. We both want to eat lots of great Christmas goodies—yum!

While we were talking about all this (and getting really excited), our friend Aleesha walked up. We told her what we were talking about. She had lots of Christmas ideas, too.

And then, while we were talking, it hit me—wouldn't it be fun to get ready for Christmas together?

I told Christine and Aleesha what I was thinking...and then we all started getting excited.

"We could have a decoration-making party!" Christine said. "I know how to make lots of stuff!"

"Maybe you could show me how to wrap a really good present! Everything I wrap ends up all wadded!" said Aleesha.

"What about a Christmas tea party...?" (That was from me. Everyone knows I love tea parties!)

We were all talking at once. Then we stopped and looked at each other, and we knew it was going to happen! All we had to do then was figure out the details—like who else would be in our club.

We decided to ask two more girls to join. Maria lives right next door to Christine and is always a lot of fun, so we knew we wanted to ask her. And Aleesha suggested Elizabeth, who is new in our school this year. "I really like her," she said. "And besides, I don't think she has very many friends yet."

That was the start of our Christmas Club. The members are Christine, Aleesha, Maria, Elizabeth, and me—Emilie Marie. Oh, and you—because you're invited, too!

The first meeting will be on the Saturday after Thanksgiving at my Grammie's house. I've already got some great ideas for things to do.

I hope you can come.

We're really going to have fun this Christmas.

Christmas Is Coming

We were all in a great mood as we climbed the steps to Grammie's little loft bedroom. Grammie said this could be our Christmas clubhouse.

"What are we going to do first?" asked Aleesha.

"Make Christmas cards," I announced. "And then Christmas lists."

Grammie had just walked in with a tray of sandwiches and cider. The hot, spicy cider smell made my nose twitch. And the sandwiches were adorable—peanut butter and jelly cut into little gingerbread people!

"Are you girls excited about Christmas?" Grammie asked.

"I can't wait!" said Elizabeth. "It seems like such a long time until then."

"You'll be surprised how fast the time flies," said Grammie. "So you'd better get started."

Before long we were working hard on our "house" Christmas cards. "These are cute," Christine said as she carefully colored a picture to go behind one of the little windows she had cut in her "house." "They're almost like the Advent calendars we have at home."

"Ad-what?" asked Aleesha.

"Advent," said Elizabeth. "It means 'coming,' like 'Christmas is coming.' "

"I like our Advent calendar because it helps me see how close it is to Christmas," said Christine. "Every day, you open another little door and read what's behind it. When all the doors are open...then it's Christmas."

"Actually," said Maria, "that might be a fun thing to talk about at our next meeting."

"Advent calendars?" asked Elizabeth.

"No," said Maria. "I mean the special things our families do every year for Christmas."

"You mean like what you have for Christmas dinner?" asked Aleesha. "In our house, we always have Great-Aunt Billie's oyster stuffing. We've had it every year for years and years. My mom says it's a tradition in our family."

"Tradition—that's it," said Elizabeth. "That's something special you do every year. It would be fun to find out about those. I like Maria's idea. We can go home and ask our moms and dads and grandmas and grandpas about our family traditions, and then we can tell about it at the next meeting. We'll be...Christmas reporters!"

So that's what we agreed to do for our next big meeting. We would meet at Maria's house and report on the special traditions we learned about.

By this time we were through making our cards, too. And now it was time for the fun part...making our Christmas wish lists.

"I already know what I want," said Maria.

"Make a list anyway," I said, "just for fun."

Christine had already filled half a page of notebook paper, but Aleesha was chewing her pencil and thinking hard.

"Here," said Grammie, who had just peeked back into the room. "I found some catalogs that might give you ideas."

After that, *all* of our lists started getting long...and longer!

"You know," Grammie said, "have you ever thought of making another list, too—a list of what you want to *give?*"

We were quiet for about three seconds. Then Christine blurted out, "I want to make a book of coupons for my mom—for taking out the trash and stuff."

COUNTING THE DAYS

It seems so long until Christmas—but there are all sorts of cute ways to help you count the days. Here are just a few!

ADVENT CALENDAR: Use the "window" idea shown in the house-card later in this chapter. Decorate a sheet of construction paper with a Christmas scene and then mark and cut 25 little doors on it. Number the doors 1-25. Now place your "door" scene over another sheet of paper. Draw a little picture or write a little saying behind every door. Glue the top sheet over the second sheet. If your doors won't stay closed, try closing them with some "sticky note" adhesive.

ACTIVITY CHAIN: Cut 25 strips of colored paper. On each slip, write a Christmas question or an activity: "Jump in a circle and sing Jingle Bells," "How many reindeer does Santa have?" or "Eat a Christmas cookie from the jar!" Join the strips into a paper chain (with the writing inside the "links") and number the links 1-25. (The last link might simply read "Have a Merry Christmas!") Hang the chain in a place where you can get to it. Each day tear off one link, answer the question or do the activity...and move one day nearer to Christmas.

CANDY ADVENT (THE SWEETEST OF ALL!): Buy 25 pieces of individually wrapped hard candy. With a permanent marker, mark the numbers 1-25 on the outside of the candies wrappers. Then tie each piece of candy to a string of red yarn or a long strip of torn fabric. Add bows if you wish. Hang your candy garland on the tree or on the wall and enjoy a piece of candy each day.

"You can also do things to help people outside your family," said Grammie. "You know Mrs. Camden around the corner has trouble keeping her lawn up since her husband died. She could use some help. And people at nursing homes are always glad to have a visit...."

Soon the ideas were really flowing. We found out that making a "give list" was as much fun as a "get list"— except we had to use our brains more!

We really felt good when we finished, though. Our Christmas Club was underway, and we had lots of great ideas for what to do next.

"But we still haven't decided on a name," I said.

"Couldn't we just be the Christmas Club?" asked Christine.

"That's boring," Elizabeth said. "How about The Christmas Elves?"

Maria frowned. "I'd rather be an angel than an elf."

"The Angels..." mused Elizabeth. "I wouldn't mind being an angel."

"Angels do good in the world," said Grammie. "That's a good name for a group of girls with a long 'give' list."

"The Angels," Christine said. "I like it."

So did I. So did everyone. And that's how we became the Angels.

A cheerful heart does good...
THE BOOK OF PROVERBS

8

A CHRISTMAS CRAFT SUPPLY KIT

You need some basic tools to make almost any craft project or recipe—including most of the ones in this book! Here is a list of things to have on hand whenever you make things:

FOR CRAFTS:

construction paper in various colors
pencils, crayons, and markers for decorating
scissors
glue stick and white glue
a ruler
newspaper or plastic to protect work surfaces

FOR RECIPES:
stove, refrigerator, and microwave
measuring cups and spoons
mixing bowls and spoons
a rolling pin
a spatula
baking pans and cookie sheets

For anything involving the stove, hot substances, or knives, ask an adult to help!

"MY HOUSE TO YOURS" CARDS

8½" x 11" sheet of light-colored construction paper
5½" x 8½" sheet of colored construction paper
crayons or markers and paper scraps
glue stick
craft knife and adult help

Fold the large sheet of construction paper in half to make the card. On the smaller sheet, draw a house with many doors and windows. The windows should have "closed" shutters as in the picture. Cut the house out and decorate it. Ask a grownup to help you cut the windows and doors open with a craft knife as shown. Then fold out the parts you cut. Position the house on the outside of your card and use your pencil to lightly trace around the inside of the windows and doors. Remove the house. You should see a little square or rectangle for every window and door. If you want, you can paste photos of your family behind the little windows or doors! Draw indoor scenes in these squares—a candle, a child looking out, a Christmas tree. Now glue the house down to the card, being sure not to glue over the doors and shutters. You should be able to open them to see what's behind. Print a greeting inside the card (like: "Merry Christmas from My House to Yours!") and sign your name.

GRAMMIE'S SPICED CIDER

This is really easy!

2 quarts of apple cider
¼ cup of brown sugar, packed tightly in the cup
1 teaspoon whole allspice
1 teaspoon whole cloves
2 cinnamon sticks
½ lemon, thinly sliced

Put all ingredients together in a pan. Heat on the stove, stirring until the sugar melts. When the cider is hot, serve it in Christmas mugs.

PBJ PEOPLE

They're really just peanut-butter-jelly sandwiches—but a lot more fun!

wheat bread
creamy peanut butter
jelly or jam (any flavor)
carrots and raisins
gingerbread man cookie cutter

First make ordinary peanut-butter-jelly sandwiches, then cut into people shapes with the cookie cutter. Use more peanut butter to glue on carrot hair, raisin faces, buttons—anything you like. You can even make shirts or dresses by spreading jelly thinly on top. Serve on a Christmas plate.

The Christmas Reporters

I showed up at Maria's house a few days later with a big bundle under my arm. While I was waiting for the door to open, Christine came up the walk.

"What's that?" she said, pointing to my bundle.

"It's part of my tradition. I don't want to open it up yet."

Just then Maria opened the door. "Hi, come on in. I hope you don't mind if we eat right away. Mama's just whipping the special Mexican hot chocolate. That's one of our traditions. You whip it with a special wooden stick called a *molinillo* that you roll back and forth in your hands."

"I think I like your traditions," I said. "The whole house smells like chocolate."

Soon we were snuggled up in the Rodriguez's den sipping the cinnamony hot chocolate.

"I think we should start our craft project first," said Maria. "This is a really fun idea—my mom showed me how to do it. She said people have been making these things for Christmas for hundreds of years, so I guess they're a tradition, too."

"What are they?"

"Pomander balls. You make them out of oranges. When you're through, you can hang them in closets to keep them smelling good. They make good presents, too. All you have to do is take an orange and stick these little cloves all over it."

"Sounds like a lot of work."

"It is, but it's fun. And we can talk about traditions while we work. Can I go first?"

Once we had learned what to do and were poking away at our oranges with the cloves, Maria told us about her traditions.

"Well, as you know, my grandparents came from Mexico," she said, "so we like to go back to their neighborhood to do special Mexican Christmas things."

"Like piñatas?" I asked.

She nodded. "But there are other things, too. Like *Las Posadas*. It's kind of like a parade and a play about Mary and Joseph looking for a place to stay so they can have Baby Jesus."

"How can it be both a parade and a play?"

"Well, it starts like a parade, with

children dressed as angels and Mary and Joseph and wise-men and all. Everybody else walks behind them and carries a candle. The whole parade goes along while everybody sings, then they finally stop at someone's door. Mary and Joseph knock on the door and ask for a room. But the person inside yells 'Go away!' "

"How rude!" said Aleesha.

"No, it's just part of the play," said Maria. "They know what is going on; they're just acting out their part. Anyway, Joseph says, 'My wife is going to have a baby, and she needs a place to rest.' Then everyone in the house yells, 'Go away!' again. So Joseph finally says that the baby is going to be the Christ Child. Then the door opens up, and everyone goes inside and has a party."

"With Mexican hot chocolate?"

"Sí. That means yes. And piñatas, too. And we also like to have *nacimientos*—manger scenes. And on Christmas Eve we go to church at midnight and afterwards have a special Christmas supper with Mama's special tamales. Those are our Christmas traditions...oh, yes, and we like to all get in the car and drive around and see the Christmas lights."

"Hey, we do that at our house, too," said Elizabeth. "And we don't put our Christmas tree up until Christmas Eve. My mom says that's an old German custom. Her family is German. She said that when her mother was little, the children didn't see the tree while it was being decorated. The tree was locked up in the living room. After supper on Christmas Eve, her grandmother would open the doors and there would be the tree, all decorated, with little candles burning on all the branches. She said it was beautiful...."

"I wouldn't want to do that," said Christine. "Helping decorate the tree is one of my favorite parts of Christmas. We have a big family party and we all work on it together."

"We do, too," said Aleesha. "Our tree is already up!"

"I want to find out about that big bundle Emilie Marie brought," said Christine.

I was glad she said that. I had really wanted to go next, anyway. I reached over and carefully unwrapped my package. It was a heavy silver candleholder with nine candles. "This is our menorah," I said. "We have it because my mother is half-Jewish."

"I thought Jewish people don't have Christmas," Aleesha said.

"Jewish people celebrate Hanukkah, which comes in December, too." I said. "It's not the same as Christmas, but there are some things that are alike. Like candles. And presents. And Hanukkah's about a miracle, just like Christmas is. It's about when the Jews had been fighting a long war and finally won. But the eternal lamp in the Temple, the one that was never supposed to go out, had gone out during the war. The people wanted to relight it, but they could only find one little jar of oil. That little jar of oil burned and burned...for eight days— that was the miracle. So we burn the candles in the menorah to help us remember—eight candles for the eight days and one for the eternal flame. Mama says that celebrating Hanukkah as well as Christmas helps our family be closer, even though we don't believe exactly the same things."

"In our family," said Aleesha, "we try to be the first one on Christmas morning to say 'Christmas Gift' to someone else. Like, if I see my brother, I try to say it to him before he can say it to me. And if I do, he's

"MERRY CHRISTMAS" AROUND THE WORLD

Christmas traditions are different in different countries, but the spirit of Christmas is the same around the world. Just for fun, here's how to say "Merry Christmas" in a lot of different languages!

Sing Dan Fae Lok. (CHINESE CANTONESE)

Joyeux Noel (FRENCH)

Frohe Weihnachten (GERMAN)

Mele Kalikimaka (HAWAIIAN)

Buon Natale (ITALIAN)

Meri Kurisumasu (JAPANESE)

God Jul (NORWEGIAN)

S nastupaiushchim Novym (RUSSIAN)

Felíz Navidad (SPANISH)

Noeliniz kutlu (TURKISH)

supposed to give me a little present, like a piece of candy. It's a lot of fun trying to beat everybody else. After all that, we open our presents."

"We open ours on Christmas Eve," put in Elizabeth. "And we like to go to church on Christmas morning. But it's Christine's turn now. What does your family do?"

"We just have a plain old Christmas," Christine said. "We put up a tree and sing carols and all that. We don't do anything really special."

"But, I know of something really special your family does," I said, "you decorate your house better than anyone in the whole neighborhood."

Christine's face lit up. "We do it all together!" she said. "It's so much fun hanging all the garlands and hanging the wreaths and putting all the ornaments on the tree. And I just thought of something else," she said. "It's sort of a new tradition. When our big

family gets together, with all the cousins, we act out a Christmas book we all like."

"That really sounds like fun," said Elizabeth. "We can never do anything like that in my family because I don't have any brothers and sisters."

Then Aleesha had an idea. "We can do that!" she said.

"Now?" said Christine. "I'm not through with my pomander yet."

"We'll never get through with these today, anyway," said Aleesha. "We can take them home and finish them."

"We have plenty of dress-up clothes," Maria said, "and I just read a book that would be fun to act out."

So the second meeting of the Christmas Club ended up a little different than we had planned. Before we knew it, we were putting together a skit to tell a legend about the first Christmas tree.

"Just one more thing," said Maria. "Before you go, my mom and I have a surprise." We all followed Maria into her kitchen, where the table was spread with a clean white tablecloth. On the counter were several dishes of bright-colored paint.

"This is the Christmas Club memory cloth," announced Maria. "We're all going to dip our hands in paint and put our handprints on the cloth and then sign our names and the date. And then we can use this tablecloth at all our meetings."

That's how the Christmas Club got its beautiful traditional tablecloth!

We were very excited as we left Maria's house.

"Don't forget," Christine called out, "that next week we meet at my house...to make fantastic, fabulous decorations!"

SPICY OLD-FASHIONED POMANDER

1 medium orange
bottle of whole cloves
⅛" wide strips of masking tape
⅛" wide ribbon
powdered cinnamon and nutmeg
powdered orris root (ask for this at a
drugstore or health food store)
1 nail

Start by placing the strips of masking tape around the orange to "reserve" space for the ribbon. Make one circle around the middle of the orange or two circles at right angles to each other. Now stick cloves into the remaining surface. Use the nail to make holes in the orange skin, then push the long pointed ends of the cloves through the holes. Leave a little space between each clove (about the size of another clove). When the fruit is full of cloves, take off the tape. Mix the spices and the orris root together in a bowl and roll the pomander in the mixture. Put the pomander in a cardboard box or paper bag somewhere where it is warm and the air circulates, like a high kitchen cabinet. Every day for a week, take it down and roll it in the spice mixture. In a few weeks it will be dry. Then you can glue on the ribbon where the masking tape was. You can even add bows, dried flowers, spices, and of course a ribbon loop for hanging.

MEXICAN HOT CHOCOLATE

2 tablets Mexican chocolate (This is chocolate
combined with sugar, almond, and
cinnamon. You can probably find it in the "ethnic"
section of a large grocery store or a Mexican market.)
¼ cup water
2 quarts milk
whipped cream
cinnamon
hand beater
or molinillo

13

Gently melt chocolate tablets in the water over very low heat. Add the milk, then heat, stirring, until just under the boiling point. Remove chocolate from heat and pour it into a jug or pitcher. Beat with the molinillo or a hand beater until foamy. Serve topped with whipped cream and a dash of cinnamon. Note: If you can't find the Mexican chocolate, use four 1-ounce squares of unsweetened chocolate. Before you beat the chocolate, add ⅔ cup sugar, ¼ teaspoon ground cinnamon, and 2 teaspoons of almond extract.

All Through the House

was Aleesha. And before long all the Angels were munching on pizza-flavored popcorn and sipping hot cranberry-apple punch.

"I thought we'd have popcorn for snacks because we're going to string popcorn for decorations," Christine said. "My mom says that popcorn and cranberry garlands are the prettiest of all. That's what families used to make when they didn't have any extra money for decorations."

"Well, that's me!" I said cheerfully. "I don't have extra money for *anything* this year. Mom says I'm supposed to make all my presents."

"Hey, I've got that covered!" said Elizabeth. "I was even thinking we could meet at my house next week and make presents together."

We all said yes to that!

"But first...we decorate," said Christine. We all started making our garlands—three pieces of non-pizza flavored popcorn, then a cranberry, then another three pieces of popcorn, and so on.

"Are you going to put your garland on the little tree in your room?" I asked Christine.

"What little tree?" asked Elizabeth.

"I'm going to have my own little Christmas tree in my room this year," Christine said, "and decorate it myself."

"Welcome to Christmas Land!" called out Christine as she let me in the door. "Fa-la-la-la and all that."

I looked around in amazement as I took off my coat. Every year the decorations in Christine's house seemed to get more wonderful. The big Christmas tree glistened with white and gold and burgundy ribbons. Little gold trees lined the mantel, and tiny white lights twinkled on the houseplants. Christine's cocker spaniel, Mickey, had on a plaid bowtie collar. He barked excitedly as he ran to meet me.

"We decorate *everything* in this house," said Christine.

"So what are we making today?" I asked.

"Lots of stuff," she said just as the doorbell rang. It

"Hey, why don't we *all* do trees?" said Aleesha. "We could have a decorating contest."

"Not a contest," said Maria. "How about a tree show? At our next meeting. We can bring our trees and show them off."

Now we were all getting into the idea.

"The trees should be creative," said Elizabeth.

"And beautiful," said Christine.

"And with homemade decorations," added Maria.

So we decided that our next meeting would be a gift-making workshop and a tree show. And then we followed Christine into the kitchen so she could show us how to make ornaments from cinnamon dough.

"You're really going to like this stuff," said Christine. "You won't believe how good it smells. You can't eat it, though."

Soon we were stirring up a cinnamon and applesauce dough and rolling it and cutting it into cookie shapes. I made a gingerbread man because I thought the brown dough looked like gingerbread. And Christine was right—it smelled wonderful.

"They'll take a couple of days to dry," Christine said as we carefully laid our ornaments out on sheets of waxed paper. "But then you can paint them to look just like little cookies...and they'll still smell great."

We left our cinnamon-dough creations drying on the kitchen counter and went back to the family room. Christine showed us how to make little redbirds from red wrapping paper, and soon our scissors and pencils were hard at work as we created our own birds. When we were through, the little birds were flying happily on their ribbon hangers.

"I *really* like them," said Maria. "Can we make some more?"

But just then Elizabeth looked at the clock. "I've got to go home. I promised my mom I would help her with dinner."

We hadn't realized it was so late! We *all* had to go.

So we gathered up our garlands, birds, and damp cinnamon cutouts. Christine and Mickey stood at the door as we walked off down the street.

The Christmas lights on the houses were already beginning to blink on, and I could smell smoke from all the chimneys.

I shivered in the frosty air, but inside I felt warm. It was really starting to feel like Christmas!

WHAT WE MADE

CINNAMON "COOKIE" CUTOUTS

These are the best-smelling ornaments in town!

large can of cinnamon (at least 3 ounces)
applesauce
waxed paper
cookie cutters in holiday shapes
rolling pin
plastic drinking straw
emery board
puff paint
ribbon for hangers

Pour almost all of the can of cinnamon into the bowl. Add several tablespoons of applesauce and mix. Keep adding applesauce a tablespoon at a time to make a thick dough. Shape the dough into a ball. Lightly dust a piece of waxed paper and the rolling pin with the rest of the cinnamon. Place the dough ball in the middle of the paper, flatten it a little with your hand, and then roll it ¼" thick. Use cookie cutters to cut out the ornaments. Dust the spatula with cinnamon and use it to lift the ornaments onto a clean piece of waxed paper. Use the drinking straw to make a hole for hanging the ornaments. Let them dry, turning them often—it may take several days. When they are completely dry, use the emery board to smooth any rough edges and decorate with puff paint. Hang with ribbons.

PIZZA POPCORN

Perfect for the popcorn you don't string on chains!

2 tablespoons grated Parmesan cheese
1 teaspoon garlic powder
1 teaspoon Italian herb
    seasoning
1 teaspoon paprika
½ teaspoon salt
2 quarts hot popcorn
olive oil spray

Put all the ingredients except the popcorn in a blender and blend on high until they're all powdered together. Put the popcorn in a big bowl, spray with olive oil spray, add cheese-spice mixture, and toss.

HOT CRANBERRY-APPLE PUNCH

You make this one cup at a time:

½ cup apple juice
½ cup cranberry juice drink
1 slice of an orange
microwave oven

Put the juices in a microwave-safe mug. Cut the orange slice in half and float the half circles in the mug. Heat in the microwave 2 minutes on high or until hot. Enjoy.

16

CHRISTMAS REDBIRDS

These look so pretty "flying" through the branches of a Christmas tree! You can make them out of any kind of wrapping paper or even from the pages of a magazine!

1

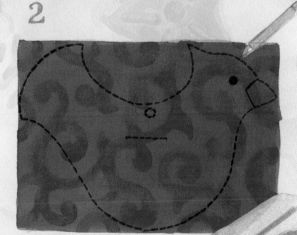

← 5"X 7"
posterboard

← 5"X 7"
red paper

two 5" x 7" pieces of shiny red wrapping paper
one 5" x 7" piece of posterboard
glue stick or rubber cement
pencil
tracing paper
scissors
craft knife and adult help
hole punch
one 4" x 6" piece of red tissue paper
thin red ribbon
black marker
yellow construction paper

2

Use glue stick or rubber cement to glue the wrapping paper to both sides of the poster paper. Let the glue dry while you trace the pattern (see last page) for the bird onto some tracing paper. (Be sure and trace the little slit in the middle where the wings will go.) Then place the tracing paper over the wrapping paper "sandwich." With your pencil, go over all the lines you traced, pressing down hard. When you lift the pencil, you should be able to see an outline of the bird on the wrapping paper. Cut out your bird along this outline. Ask a grownup to cut along the wing slit with a craft knife. Also, use the hole punch to punch a hole right over the slit. To make the wings, fold the red tissue paper like a fan and push the pleated paper through the slit on the bird's back. Cut a 9-12" piece of thin ribbon and pull it through the hole to make a hanger. Draw in the bird's face with a black marker. If you wish, cut two little triangles of yellow construction paper and glue them on to make the beak.

3

**4"X 6"
tissue paper**

4

The Heavenly Workshop

"You're almost the last one here," Elizabeth told me when she answered the door. "Now all we need is Aleesha. Is that your tree? You can put it over on this table. We're going to start making gifts first."

I placed my little decorated tree carefully on a table next to three lumpy, mysterious objects— one covered with a pillowcase, another draped in a towel, and another one hidden in a plastic garbage bag. My tree was covered by a plastic bag too. We wanted the Tree Show to be a surprise!

Elizabeth led me down the hall to a big, cheerful kitchen. Christine and Maria were standing by a wooden table measuring cups of dried beans into a big roasting pan.

"Hey, Emilie Marie, come on in," said Christine. "We're just starting on our bean bags."

"We don't need that many beans to make beanbags!" I said, peering into the big pan. It was full of all kinds of beans—black ones, brown ones, speckled ones, and even little peas.

"This isn't the kind of beanbag you play with," Elizabeth said. "It's a bag of beans that people can make into soup. We're going to put all these beans into plastic bags and add recipes for making soup with the beans. My mom says it's the kind of gift that everybody likes—food!"

Umm, food! That sounded pretty good to me, too. For this meeting, we had decided to eat dinner together, and the warm smells coming from the stove were already making my mouth water.

It didn't take long to scoop the beans into plastic bags. We were copying the recipes when we heard a car in the driveway.

"That's Aleesha," said Elizabeth, running to the door.

It was Aleesha all right. She was carrying her little tree—not wrapped up at all.

"What's wrong?" we all chorused.

"Oh, it's OK." She waved at her dad as he backed out of the driveway. "It's just that my little sister Marti knocked over our tree and broke the angel that goes on top. And Mama got upset, and the baby started crying, and Daddy was running late to bring me here...."

"You know," she added as she handed Elizabeth her coat, "I really like Christmas, but sometimes it's just crazy. My mom was sorry she was upset; she's just got too much to do."

"I know what you mean," Maria said. "My mom's like that too these days."

And then I had an idea.

"Hey, maybe this is the time for us to *really* be Christmas angels. Maybe we can *help* our moms get everything done. We can help do chores...or we can babysit."

"I have to do that anyway," said Maria.

"Yeah, but this'll be more fun because we'll do it together. One afternoon we can help at Aleesha's house, and then we can go to Christine's house, and so on. And we can work together to help with whatever needs to be done."

We had finished our beanbags and were busy making spicy Christmas potpourri when Elizabeth's mom came into the kitchen. "Are you girls ready to eat?"

We finished our little jars of potpourri. Then we all ate big bowls of yummy bean soup—I never even knew I liked bean soup—and big pieces of warm gingerbread. And then we were ready for the big Christmas Tree Show!

Happy are the kind...
THE BOOK OF MATTHEW

WHAT WE MADE

"BEANBAG" SOUP MIX

This recipe will make enough for eight gift bags.

2 cups of each of the following: black beans, butter beans or large limas, pinto beans, navy beans, pearl barley, split green peas, small lima beans, red beans, Great Northern beans, lentils

Combine beans in a large container; mix well. Divide mixture evenly into eight plastic bags—about 2½ cups in each. Tie the bags with ribbons or twist-ties and attach the Yummy Bean Bag Soup recipe.

YUMMY BEAN BAG SOUP

1 package "Beanbag" Soup Mix
1 large onion, chopped
1 29-ounce can tomatoes
2 teaspoons chili pepper
1 clove crushed garlic
juice of 1 lemon
salt and pepper to taste

Wash beans thoroughly and place in large pot. Add enough water to cover beans by 2 inches. Boil 2 minutes and let stand 1 hour. Drain and add 2 quarts of water and ½ pound ham or ham hocks and simmer 1½ to 2 hours, covered. Add the rest of the ingredients and simmer 30 minutes or until beans are tender. Makes 10-12 big servings.

CITRUS SPICE POTPOURRI

Sweet-smelling potpourri usually has to sit for weeks before it's ready, but this quick kind uses fruit peelings and spices from the kitchen. We put it in baby-food jars and decorated the top with lacy doilies and ribbons.

9 oranges or tangerines
9 lemons
1 cup whole cloves
1 cup whole allspice
20 cinnamon sticks, broken
20 bay leaves, crumbled
8-10 baby-food jars
small paper or cloth doilies
satin ribbon
small dried flowers

Preheat over to 175° or "warm." Ask an adult to help you peel the oranges and lemons carefully with a vegetable peeler. Be sure to remove only the orange and yellow peel, not the white stuff underneath. Tear the peel into 1" pieces and spread them on paper towels in a baking pan or cookie sheet. Dry them in the heated oven for about 1½ hours, stirring them around occasionally. Then leave them out to dry some more—about 24 hours. When the pieces of orange and lemon are dry, mix them in a big bowl with all the other spices. Put the mixture into the little jars and screw the lids on tightly. Put a doily on top of the jar and tie with a pretty ribbon. Add a little card with the instructions about how to use.

CITRUS SPICE POTPOURRI

To use, remove the lid and put in a warm place to fragrance the room. For more fragrance, put 2 tbls of this mixture in a cup and add boiling water.

THE BIG CHRISTMAS TREE SHOW

Here's what we saw when we uncovered our Christmas trees. Each tree was different! (Maybe you could do one for your room!)

glue

Christine's Lacy Tree

Christine decorated her whole tree from one package of paper doilies! She just cut the middles from a stack of doilies to make a stack of "snowflakes" and a stack of lacy "doughnuts." The "snowflakes" became ornaments (she glued on loops of thread as hangers) and even a star for the top of the tree. The "doughnuts" became a garland. Christine just cut them in half and glued the half-circles together as shown to make a wavy, lacy garland. Pretty!

Elizabeth's Horse Tree

Elizabeth's a real horse lover, so she decorated her tree with little plastic horses! She just tied ribbons around their middles and tied them on the tree with big bows. She put little paper saddles on, too, and a toy western sheriff's star on top!

Aleesha's Recycling Tree

Aleesha made all her decorations from her family's recycling bin (her family really cares about the environment)! She used the color Sunday comics to make a fun paper chain and candy cups. She also put red and green glitter on bottle caps to add some sparkle to her tree.

Maria's Bird Tree

Remember how Maria liked our paper birds? Well, her tree was covered with colorful, shiny paper birds made out of all different kinds of Christmas wrapping paper. She folded other pieces of paper into little paper fans and tucked those in the branches, too.

Emilie Marie's Tea Tree

I love tea parties, and I have lots of little tea sets and tea things people have given me. So I made my tree a tea tree. I used ribbon and tape to tie on little cups, little silver spoons, and even some tea bags in their paper wrappers.

A Peppermint Tea

It was almost three o'clock—and I couldn't wait! Our special "peppermint tea" party was about to begin.

All month, even while we were making decorations and gifts and learning about traditions, we had been planning this party. We had sent out invitations to every girl in our class, and only two had said they couldn't come. In just a few minutes our friends would be ringing our doorbell— each dressed in red and white and carrying a brightly wrapped present. We had a special plan for those presents!

Christine, Maria, Aleesha, and Elizabeth had been at my house since early that morning, putting the finishing touches on the food and the decorations. And everything was *beautiful*.

In the dining room, a crepe-paper garland swooped around the edges of the white tablecloth, held in place by pretty paper "peppermint" carnations. The table centerpiece was a wreath of ivy holding candy-striped candles in several sizes, with more carnations tucked around for color. There were trays and trays of yummy tea party food. And our big teakettle was simmering on the stove, all ready to start a big pot of tangy-cool peppermint tea.

There would be too many of us to have our tea around the dining table, so we had set up card tables in the living room. We had even made red-and-white placemats, and the white paper napkins were tied with pretty red ribbons.

"Ding-dong!" The doorbell told me someone was here already. Quickly I ran over to turn on the stereo. Beautiful violin music filled the air as Christine opened the door. There stood our friend Brittany, dressed in a white turtleneck and a red skirt, and holding a brightly wrapped package. "Merry Christmas!" we all called out. Our wonderful, festive Peppermint Tea had begun.

We had so much fun that day! We put the presents under our big tree and talked while the tea brewed. We ate and drank, using our very best party manners. We played "Christmas Carol" charades—with each person trying to act out the name of a favorite Christmas song. Our Christmas Club performed our Christmas skit, the one we had made up at our second meeting.

And then...this is the best part! We had asked everyone

to bring a nice, new, beautiful, fun toy—but we weren't going to keep them!

After we had eaten and played our games, we all drew names and gave the wrapped toys to each other. We opened them up and oohed and aahed and even played with them a little.

And then...we all piled into our car and Christine's mom's van and delivered those nice new toys to the "Toys for Kids" barrels down at the mall. The barrel was only half full when we got there, and it was overflowing when we left.

Everyone was smiling and full of the Christmas spirit when we said goodbye to our guests at the door. Everybody said they had a great time.

Now the next great thing we had to look forward to was...Christmas!

WHAT WE MADE

OUR CANDY-STRIPED INVITATIONS

5½" x 8½" piece of heavy white paper
red marker with a square "chisel tip" that writes both thick and thin
thin black or red marker
a ruler

Fold the white paper in half to make a notecard. Open it out again and lay it on some newspapers with the "front" of the notecard closest to you. This is what you will decorate. Turn the ruler at an angle and use it to draw thick diagonal lines across the card. For each stripe, line the ruler up against the line you just drew, and be sure to stop at the fold. Now go back and draw thin diagonal lines between the thick ones, as shown in the picture. They don't have to be exactly in the center between the thick lines, but try to keep them lined up straight. If you wish, draw a little red heart or a teacup and saucer in the middle of the wide stripe at the bottom. Fold the card again. Inside, write the important details about the tea: what kind of party it is, who is giving it, where and when it will be held.

You might also give your phone number and ask your friends to RSVP, which means, "please let me know if you can come." Also include special information about what to wear and what to bring.

PAPER PEPPERMINT CARNATIONS

red and white tissue paper cut into lots of 3" x 3" squares
florist's wire or long green pipe cleaners
green florist's tape

Make a stack of five squares of tissue, alternating red and white. Fold the stack back and forth like a fan, then pinch the folded stack in the middle and wrap a piece of wire around it, twisting the wire together below the paper to make a stem. With scissors, cut a row of little notches into each end of the folded stack. Then, one by one, pull apart the individual squares of tissue paper to form petals. Fluff out the petals to finish your flower.

To decorate our table, we made a bunch of these carnations. We also made some plain red and white ones. We twisted red and white crepe paper streamers together and draped them around the edge of the table, holding them to the edge of the tablecloth with pins. Then we taped a few of our carnations over the pins to hide them.

23

CANDY-STRIPED CANDLE CENTERPIECE

white candles in varying heights and sizes
simple candle holders
sticks of striped peppermint candy
    (or candy canes) as long as the
    candle is high
masking tape
rubber bands
Christmas ribbon
small pine branches,
    vines of ivy, or silk garland of greenery
paper "peppermint" carnations

Wrap a few strips of masking tape sticky side out, around a candle, tape in place. Unwrap candy sticks and place them around the candle, pressing them against the masking tape. Hold the candy in place with 1 or 2 rubber bands, and tie ribbon around the candle to hide the rubber bands. If you can't find candy sticks in the sizes you need, just use red acrylic paint and a wide brush to paint red stripes onto your white candle, as shown. Use masking tape to make your stripes straight or go wild and paint them in all squiqqly!

To make the centerpiece, put the candles in their holders and group them together in the middle of the table. Arrange the branches or vines around the candles' bases to make a wreath. Tuck some paper carnations here and there in the wreath.

CANDY SWIRL PLACEMATS

12" x 18" piece of shiny red Christmas paper
    (or construction paper)
two 12" x 18" pieces of waxed paper
12" x 18" sheet of white construction paper
red and white crayon shavings made with a crayon
    sharpener or a plastic knife with sawtooth edges
iron and ironing board
rubber cement

Turn the piece of wrapping paper shiny side down and draw a line 2" from all four edges. Cut carefully along this line to make a red frame. Cover the ironing board with newspapers. Place the first sheet of waxed paper on top of them with the waxed (shinier) side facing up. Sprinkle the crayon shavings over the waxed paper. Lay the second piece of waxed paper (shiny side down) on top of the crayon shavings and press the waxed paper "sandwich" with an iron set at its very lowest heat. The heat from the iron will stick the two sheets of waxed paper together and melt the crayon bits into an interesting swirly design. To put the placemat together, start with the piece of white construction paper. Spread rubber cement around its edges and carefully lay the ironed waxed paper on top. Put more rubber cement around the edge of the waxed paper and lay your red "frame" on top of that. Press down the edges all around, and let the rubber cement dry.

24

Our Menu

Chicken-Pecan Angels
Candy-cane Cookies
Emilie Marie's Triple
Chocolate Cake
Peppermint Ice Cream
Peppermint Tea (of course!)

CHICKEN-PECAN ANGELS

white and wheat bread slices
3 boneless, skinless chicken
breasts, cooked and
chopped coarsely
½ cup finely chopped pecans
¼ cup finely chopped celery
½ cup mayonnaise
butter

Butter bread slices. Mix chicken, pecans, celery, and mayonnaise. Make sandwiches, using about 3 tablespoons of the pecan mixture on each sandwich. Chill sandwiches, then use cookie cutters to cut into angel shapes. Wrap in waxed paper until ready to use.

CANDY CANE COOKIES

1½ cups powdered sugar
1 cup butter, softened
1 teaspoon vanilla
1 egg
½ teaspoon salt
1 teaspoon baking soda
2½ cups flour
1 teaspoon red food coloring

Mix sugar, butter, vanilla, and egg in one bowl. Mix dry ingredients together, then add to sugar/butter mixture. Stir until dough forms a ball. Divide dough in half. Add red food coloring to half the dough and mix. Cover each ball of dough with waxed paper and refrigerate at least an hour. Heat oven to 350˚. Take one tablespoon of plain dough and roll between fingers until about the thickness of a pencil. Do the same thing with a tablespoon of red dough. Place the two "pencils" side by side and twist together, then bend the end to make a cane. Bake on ungreased cookie sheet 8 to 11 minutes until cookies are set but not brown.

TRIPLE CHOCOLATE FUDGE CAKE

cooking spray or oil
1 small package chocolate pudding mix
(the kind you cook)
milk (to prepare pudding)
1 box chocolate cake mix
½ cup semisweet chocolate pieces
½ cup chopped nuts
peppermint ice cream

Use oil or cooking spray to grease a 13" x 9" x 2" pan. Prepare pudding mix as directed on the package. Blend the cake mix (dry mix) into the hot pudding. The mixture will be very thick. Pour cake into prepared pan and sprinkle with chocolate pieces and nuts. Bake 30 to 35 minutes at 350˚. Cool 5 minutes and cut into 2" squares. Arrange on cake plate or doily-lined tray. Serve with a scoop of peppermint ice cream.

Here We Come A-Caroling

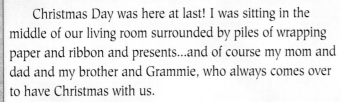

and the shepherds and the little baby Jesus. Then we sang some Christmas carols, and then it was time for bed.

I had a hard time going to sleep. I always do on Christmas Eve. But then, before I knew it, it was morning, and we were tiptoeing in to see what was waiting under the Christmas tree and tucked in our stockings. I got a big stuffed moose and also a diary—I'm going to write in it every day.

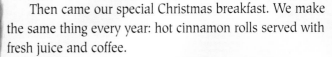

Then came our special Christmas breakfast. We make the same thing every year: hot cinnamon rolls served with fresh juice and coffee.

And then we all sat in the living room and opened presents. Mom loved her pomander. Grammie loved her potpourri. Dad loved the cinnamon ornament I made him to hang in his car as an air freshener. My brother *really* loved the little coupon book I made him—each coupon said that I would help him with one of his chores.

And of course, I liked all my presents, too. The best one of all was from Grammie.

"I couldn't wrap your present, Emilie Marie," she said. "It wouldn't let me." And while I was sitting there wondering what that could mean she went down the hall and came back carrying a silver-and-black striped kitten.

Can you guess what I named my special, adorable present? Why, Angel, of course. And I couldn't wait to tell my Angel friends about her.

Christmas Day was here at last! I was sitting in the middle of our living room surrounded by piles of wrapping paper and ribbon and presents...and of course my mom and dad and my brother and Grammie, who always comes over to have Christmas with us.

It had already been a wonderful day...and it was only ten o'clock in the morning!

Actually, our wonderful day had started last night, when we all gathered near the tree to read the story of the very first Christmas from the Bible. I felt so warm sitting there in my pajamas while my dad read about the angels

We'd all agreed that Christmas Eve and Christmas Day were for spending with our families. But I couldn't help thinking about my Angel friends as I sat there dangling a piece of Christmas ribbon for my little kitty to pounce on. I hoped their Christmas was as wonderful as mine was!

I'd find out later in the afternoon. After Christmas dinner was over, Mom had said I could go by all their houses to give each of my friends a special present I had made...an angel ornament that told why I thought each one was special. Right now, though, it was time to start making dinner.

As usual, my mom was in charge of the turkey and dressing. My dad made a big salad with everything. My brother helped Grammie put together the green-bean casserole. And I was in charge of setting the table—with our pretty white tablecloth and the centerpiece Grammie and I had made out of green pine branches and red apples and white candles...and white napkins tied up with my Christmas Rose Napkin Rings.

It was a fantastic dinner, just like always. Finally, it was time to take my presents over to my Angel friends.

First, Mom and I drove to Christine's house. She loved her little angel ornament, which said: "You're an angel because you always listen to me" And she wanted to go next door with me to deliver Maria's ornament. It said, "You're an angel because you've got a kind heart and helpful hands."

Guess what Maria and Christine wanted to do then? They each got permission to go with me and Mom to deliver Aleesha's angel! It said: "You're an angel because you're honest and truthful and funny."

Well, since the Christmas Club was almost all together now, it just seemed natural for us all to show up at Elizabeth's house and tell her together: "You're an angel because you're smart and creative and have great ideas."

"You know what?" said Elizabeth's mother as she admired the ornament. "Our family always likes to go caroling together on Christmas night, then enjoy some Christmas cookies and hot wassail punch. Would you girls and your families like to go with us?"

And we did! We made a few phone calls, and soon a whole group of us were strolling down Elizabeth's street holding candles and flashlights and little books of Christmas carols. We made a pretty good choir—moms and dads and grammies and brothers and sisters and cousins, all gazing up at the stars and singing every Christmas song we could think of—from "Silent Night" to "Jingle Bells" to "Up on the Housetop"—and, finally, "Angels We Have Heard on High."

"That was the very best one," I said softly when we had finished. And we all nodded. All those "glorrrr—iii—aas" and the beautiful, starry sky had left us thinking of that beautiful cold night so long ago...the very first Christmas night. We were all quiet for a minute.

And then Aleesha said, "Well, that's not what Elizabeth's neighbors are going to be singing."

"What are you talking about?" I asked.

"Well," she said, "They're not going to be singing 'Angels We Have Heard on High...' "

"I get it!" said Christine. "They're going to be singing, 'Angels We Have Heard...Outside!' "

Pattern 1

Pattern 2

Pattern 3

WHAT WE MADE

CHRISTMAS ROSE NAPKIN RINGS

red felt
green felt
tracing paper

FOLD

FOLD

Trace the three patterns on this page onto tracing paper (you'll need to use the copy machine to enlarge them by 200%). Fold a piece of red felt. Place patterns 1 and 2 on the felt with the straight side on the fold. Draw around the patterns with a pencil and then cut them out (don't cut the fold!) Do the same thing with pattern 3 on a piece of green felt. Be sure and cut the little holes in patterns 2 and 3! Look at the piece of felt you cut from pattern 1 (leave it folded). It should have the fold on one end and a kind of heart shape on the other. Pinch together the folded end and push it through the hole in pattern 2. Then push it through the hole in pattern 3.

Push 2 and 3 up against the "heart" to form the rose. Open out the folded end you just pushed through. That's the loop for your napkin.

"YOU'RE AN ANGEL" ORNAMENT

light posterboard
tracing paper
Christmas wrapping
paper
snapshot of person the
ornament is for
glue
pen or marker
gold or silver Christmas ribbon

Photo →

Trace the outline of the angel from the last page onto tracing paper. Glue pretty and bright-colored Christmas wrapping paper to one side of a 6½" by 5½" piece of poster-board. Trace the angel outline onto the piece and cut out. On a white or gold-colored doily, trace and cut out the angel again, this time cutting out the heart in the center of the angel. Glue the doily onto the wrapping paper side of the posterboard (the wrapping paper will show through the doily). Cut out a picture of your friend's face and glue it in the center of the heart. Use a hole punch to put holes in the wings (see pattern) and tie a pretty ribbon to make a hanger for the tree. On the back of the ornament, write the words "You're an angel because..." Then write in some words that describe the person you're making the ornament for.

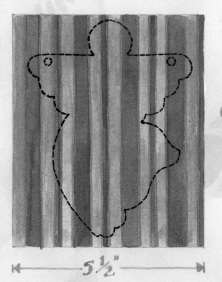

6½"

5½"

CAROLERS' WASSAIL BOWL

In the olden days in England, carolers went from house to house singing and drinking a punch called "wassail." This punch is great for serving carolers...or yourself!

1 gallon apple cider
1 large can pineapple juice
1 cup orange spice herb tea
1 tablespoon whole cloves
1 tablespoon whole allspice
2 cinnamon sticks
square piece of muslin cloth
small piece of string

Mix the juices together in a big pot or a crockery pot. Put the spices in the middle of a little square of muslin cloth and tie with a string into a little bundle. Put the spice bag in the pot and let the whole thing simmer 4 to 8 hours. Add water if it gets too strong.

29

It's Not Over Yet

The morning after Christmas, I woke up feeling happy and sad all at once. Happy because it had been such a wonderful, fun, special Christmas. And sad because it wouldn't be Christmas again for another whole year!

"I'm going to miss having a Christmas club," I told Angel as I wiggled my toes under the covers for her to jump on.

I told Elizabeth the same thing when she called a little later. And she said, "But Christmas isn't over yet!"

I didn't have a clue what she was talking about.

"You know that song," she said, 'The Twelve Days of Christmas'?"

"With the partridge and pear tree?" I asked.

"Uh-huh," she said. "Well, the twelve days of Christmas starts today."

I still didn't know what she was talking about.

"It's an old, old way to celebrate Christmas," Elizabeth explained. "But a lot of people still do it, especially in countries like England. The idea is that the Christmas season doesn't really get started until Christmas day, and it goes on until January 6. That's supposed to be when the three wise men finally get to Bethlehem. January 6 is called Epiphany, and my mom says that in some countries children get their gifts on Epiphany instead of Christmas...because the wise men brought gifts to baby Jesus. And a lot of people have parties and stuff. That's the Twelfth Day of Christmas. So anyway, if a lot of other people celebrate twelve days of Christmas, why can't we?"

"You mean we can keep on being the Angels for twelve more days?"

"I guess we'll be angels in a pear tree!" Elizabeth giggled.

That began our Twelve Days of Christmas—Angel style. We didn't have any partridges or pear trees, but we got together every day for at least one special activity. It was a great way to spend our Christmas vacation—having fun, and helping others, too.

Here's what we did on our twelve days:

The First Day of Christmas (December 26): In England, this is called "Boxing Day," and it's a day when people give presents to the people who help them. We decided to have a Boxing Day for the birds! We smeared pine cones with peanut butter, rolled them in birdseed, and hung them on our trees for the birds to enjoy.

The Second Day of Christmas (December 27): We finished *all* our thank-you notes together and then watched a video.

The Third Day of Christmas (December 28): We went to a nursing home and sang our Christmas carols for the people who lived there. They loved it!

The Fourth Day of Christmas (December 29): We spread a big puzzle out on a card table in our Christmas clubhouse and spent the afternoon working on it. Grammie helped, but we still had to come back the next day to finish.

The Fifth Day of Christmas (December 30): We "rang out the old year" by helping each other get rid of old stuff we didn't want. Then we all went skating.

The Sixth Day of Christmas (December 31): This was New Year's Eve, so we all went over to Aleesha's for a New Year's Eve sleepover. We ate New Year snacks and had a board game marathon. We also made kazoos, which we blew at midnight. (Aleesha's mom let us stay up!)

The Seventh Day of Christmas (January 1): Happy New Year! We all wrote New Year's letters to ourselves to be sealed up and opened next New Year's Eve.

The Eighth Day of Christmas (January 2): The Christmas Club turned into a "take down the tree brigade." We went from house to house and worked together to help our moms and dads take down our family Christmas trees.

The Ninth Day of Christmas (January 3): Christine's dad took us for a long hike in the park. It was cold, but fun!

The Tenth Day of Christmas (January 4): We had a winter carnival for the kids in our neighborhood. There wasn't any snow, so we ran races, played games, jumped rope, and served hot cider to help everyone warm up.

The Eleventh Day of Christmas (January 5): We just sat around and sipped hot chocolate and read books. It was one of our last days of Christmas vacation—and of the Christmas Club. We did make up a list of things we want to do for next year's Christmas Club.

The Twelfth Day of Christmas (January 6): We had an Epiphany Party just for us. Elizabeth told us that in many places they have special cakes called King Cakes (after the Three Kings) with a bean, a coin, or a little toy baked right in. The person who finds the bean in his or her piece of cake gets to be king for the day.

Well, Elizabeth made King Cupcakes for our party, and she really surprised us. She said she was going to put a bean in one of the cupcakes, but instead she put a bean in every one! So we were all queens for the day—a perfect end to the very best Christmas we had ever had!

WHAT WE MADE

"FOR THE BIRDS" BOXING DAY TREATS

pine cones
peanut butter
birdseed
thin cord or wire for hanging

Start by tying a piece of thin cord or wire around the top of the cone so you can hang it. Coat the pine cone with peanut butter, working it into the inside of the cone. Then roll the whole thing in birdseed and hang outside. You can do the same thing with big pretzels. Birds love them!

NEW YEAR'S KAZOOS

toilet paper tube
waxed paper
rubber band
colored tissue
    paper
metallic star
    stickers

Fold the waxed paper over one end of the tube and hold it in place with the rubber band. Poke a small pin hole in the center of the waxed paper. Then cut a piece of tissue paper as wide as the tube and about 12" long. Cover tube with tissue paper by wrapping the tissue several times around the roll and gluing or taping the end down. Decorate kazoo with star stickers and hum into the open end. The kazoo should make a funny buzzing noise to celebrate the New Year.

KING CUPCAKES

Purple, green, and gold are the traditional colors for an Epiphany King Cake.

1 box yellow cake mix
muffin liners (we used
    gold metallic ones!)
1 can cherry, apple, or pineapple pie filling

1 can white frosting
yellow, green, and
    purple colored sugar
cinnamon
1 pea or bean

Make cake mix according to package directions. Line muffin tin with liners. Pour half of batter into muffin tins. Put 1 tablespoon pie filling in the center of each half-filled cupcake cup. Also, put a pea or bean in one of the cups. Fill cups with the rest of the batter. Bake as directed. When cool, frost with canned frosting. Put each color of sugar in a little bowl and mix with a little cinnamon. Sprinkle stripes of yellow, green, and purple sugar on cupcakes.

"RING IN THE NEW YEAR" SNACKS

1 cup granola
½ cup unsalted sunflower seeds
2 tablespoons toasted wheat germ
½ cup raisins
1 one-ounce package hot-cocoa mix
¾ cup crunchy peanut butter
½ cup honey
1 cup shredded coconut

Mix granola, seeds, wheat germ, raisins, and cocoa mix. Add peanut butter and honey, mix. Shape into balls and roll in coconut.

Love and joy come to you,
And to your wassail to!
And God bless you and send you
A happy New Year,
And God send you a Happy New Year!

TRADITIONAL ENGLISH CAROL

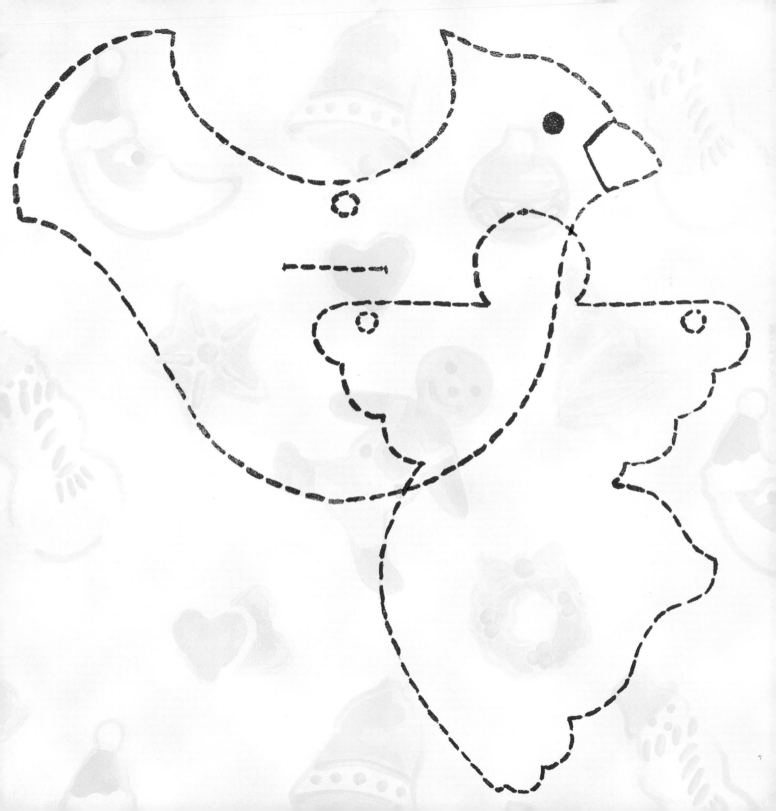